LYNXES

Henry Randall

PowerKiDS
press™

New York

Published in 2011 by The Rosen Publishing Group, Inc.
29 East 21st Street, New York, NY 10010

First Edition

Editor: Joanne Randolph
Book Design: Ashley Burrell

Photo Credits: Cover © www.iStockphoto.com/Eduard Kyslynskyy; pp. 5, 15 iStockphoto/Thinkstock; pp. 6, 24 (left) © S. Meyers/age fotostock; pp. 9, 24 (right) © Christian Heinrich/age fotostock; pp. 10–11, 21 Shutterstock.com; p. 12 Gerry Ellis/Getty Images; pp. 16–17, 24 (center right) © www.iStockphoto.com/Albert Mendelewski; pp. 18, 22, 24 (center left) Jupiterimages/Photos.com/Thinkstock.

Library of Congress Cataloging-in-Publication Data

Randall, Henry, 1972-
 Lynxes / by Henry Randall. — 1st ed.
   p. cm. — (Cats of the wild)
 Includes bibliographical references and index.
 ISBN 978-1-4488-2517-2 (library binding) — ISBN 978-1-4488-2619-3 (pbk.) —
ISBN 978-1-4488-2620-9 (6-pack)
 1. Lynx—Juvenile literature. I. Title.
 QL737.C23R36 2011
 599.75'3—dc22
                                    2010019788

Manufactured in the United States of America

CPSIA Compliance Information: Batch #WW11PK: For Further Information contact Rosen Publishing, New York, New York at 1-800-237-9932

Contents

Lynxes are wild cats that live in forests around the world. These cats are great climbers.

Lynxes have **fur** that keeps them warm in cold weather. Do you see the spots on these lynxes' fur?

Lynxes are known for the black **tufts** of fur on the tips of their ears. These hairs help them hear.

Lynxes rest in the forest during the day. They come out to find food when it gets dark.

Lynxes can climb to high places to look for food. Lynxes eat mostly hares or rabbits.

The lynx's eyes are some of its best tools. It counts on its eyesight for hunting animals.

The lynx does not have a long **tail**, as some other cats do.

Lynx **kittens** are born in the spring. They stay with their mother for about one year.

This lynx waits quietly in the grass for its dinner. When an animal gets close, the lynx jumps on it.

Lynxes can jump, run, and climb. What else do you want to know about them?

Words to Know

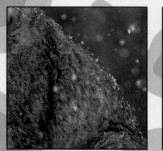
fur

kittens

tail

tufts

Index

Web Sites

Due to the changing nature of Internet links, PowerKids Press has developed an online list of Web sites related to the subject of this book. This site is updated regularly. Please use this link to access the list:
www.powerkidslinks.com/cotw/lynxes/